EXOTIC ASIA
Singapore

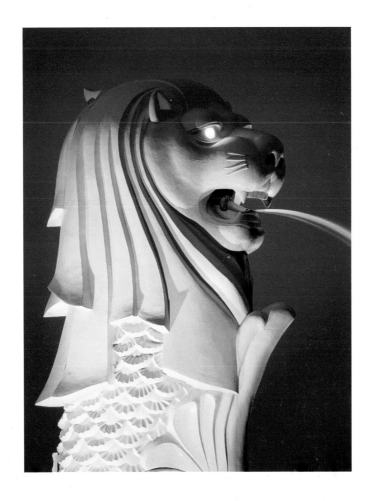

R.IAN LLOYD PRODUCTIONS

EXOTIC ASIA
Singapore

Photography by R. Ian Lloyd
Text by Joseph R. Yogerst

R. IAN LLOYD PRODUCTIONS

The most enduring (and endearing) symbol of Singapore's colonial past is Raffles Hotel, opened in 1887 by the Sarkies brothers. The hotel quickly became a hub of European life in the colony as locals flocked here for tea on the terrace, sundowners at the Long Bar and flamboyant social functions in the ballroom. Many of the world's most famous writers have also stayed at Raffles  including Somerset Maugham, Joseph Conrad, Noel Coward, Hermann Hesse and James Michener.

Singapore was little more than a mosquito-infested swamp when an ambitious young Englishman by the name of Stamford Raffles stepped ashore along the banks of the Singapore River in 1819. He brokered a deal with the local Malay chieftain and the Sultan of Johor to develop a British trading station on the little-known island as a counterweight to Portuguese, Dutch and French influence in South East Asia. From the very start, Raffles was determined to establish a settlement that would attract talented immigrants from all around Asia and a multiracial society that would grease the wheels of his great entrepreneurial gateway. His original town plan included Chinese, Indian, Malay and  European quarters on either side of the river, neighbourhoods that largely persist into modern times. Raffles' vision became the very cornerstone of Singapore society; his dream became the dream of the hundreds of thousands who followed in his footsteps. During the 19th century, Singapore would evolve into one of the crown jewels of the British Empire, hundreds of ships arrayed along a waterfront that displayed some of the world's finest colonial architecture. While many of the old structures (like the domed Supreme Court Building) retain their bygone functions, many of the colonial gems have been converted to other uses in modern times—restaurants, museums, performance spaces, boutiques and galleries.

 It may seem rather odd to have a Chinatown in a city that is predominantly Chinese, but the Singapore district harkens back to the early 1820s, when Sir Stamford Raffles drew up a revolutionary town plan that included four distinct ethnic quarters. Chinese immigrants were allotted space on the south bank of the Singapore River, where Chinatown lingers today, wedged between Boat Quay, the Financial District and the Tanjong Pagar dock area. In bygone days, Chinatown was a slum where immigrants jammed together in dilapidated shophouses and made a living as coolies, servants or common labourers. Even though Singapore was under British control, Chinatown was dominated by secret societies and clan associations representing the different ethnic groups—Hokkien, Teochew, Cantonese, Hainanese and Hakka people—who had nothing in common other than a desire to find a new and better life in Singapore. By the end of its first century, the neighbourhood was rife with opium dens and brothels. After independence in the 1960s, land reclamation and development of the Financial District separated Chinatown from its traditional ties with the waterfront. The area was set for wholesale demolition when advocates of historical preservation convinced the government to refurbish rather than destroy the old shophouses.

Officially dubbed "Chinese Baroque," Singapore's ubiquitous shophouse architecture is a synthesis of several distinct styles brought together by British rule in the East. A typical shophouse might include Georgian balustrades, arches and cornices, Malay wooden doors and window shutters, or Chinese roof tiles and banisters adorned with intricately carved dragonheads. The facades are narrow, but they are actually quite spacious, rising two or three stories above street level and stretching deep into the lot.  Born of the colonial era, the name derives from the fact that many had shops on the ground floor and living quarters above. Many of the shophouses in Chinatown and Tanjong Pagar were once used for opium dens, "death houses" where the elderly went to spend their final days, and "remittance houses" that catered to illiterate immigrants sending money back home to relatives in China. Every historic neighbourhood—Little India, Kampong Glam, Geylang Serai, Emerald Hill—sports its own version of the shophouse. Spurred by Singapore's economic boom and cultural nostalgia, they have been painstakingly restored in recent times, converted into modern shops and restaurants. Shophouse-style homes in residential areas like Emerald Hill—once spurned as hopelessly outdated—have become trendy places to live in recent years and are now among the island's most expensive properties.

Many of the island's landmark colonial-era buildings have been converted into museums that are among the finest of their kind in Southeast Asia. The Asian Civilizations Museum—divided between Empress Place and the old Tao Nan School—is a treasure chest of ancient Chinese, Indian, Thai and Indonesian art, antiques and artefacts. The Singapore History Museum (left) started life in 1886 as a place to display the natural and anthropological collections amassed by Stamford Raffles. The National Art Museum is situated in the wonderfully restored St. Joseph's Institute.

Singapore's darkest hour came in February of 1942 when Japanese forces captured the island from British Empire troops. Not long after their attack on Pearl Harbour, the Japanese crippled the Singapore-based British fleet during a battle on the South China Sea, paving the way for invasion of the Malay Peninsula. Amphibious landings along the island's north coast kicked off the Battle of Singapore, which waged for seven bloody days. Allied forces, cut off from reinforcement and supplies, eventually surrendered in what Winston Churchill termed "the worst disaster and largest capitulation in British history." The Japanese Occupation—during which thousands of Singaporeans were butchered—lasted until August of 1945, when atom bombs were dropped on the Japanese mainland. The formal Japanese surrender took place in what is now the Supreme Court (right), an event commemorated in wax at the Surrender Chamber on Sentosa Island (above).

Thousands of trishaws once bustled about Singapore's streets, but their number has dwindled to no more than a handful in recent years. After independence, the government nearly outlawed them as road hazards. But a few survive for the amusement of tourists, quaint reminders of a time when transportation—and life in general—was much slower. Nowadays the best places to spot them  are the quiet lanes of Chinatown, where the drivers often take time out for a shave or a snack in their favourite *kopi tiam* (coffee shop).

Ancient ways and means continue to thrive in Chinatown and other ethnic neighbourhoods. For some prized songbirds, Sunday morning means an outing with their owner to special coffee houses where they can demonstrate their warbling skills. One of the world's oldest hobbies, the training of songbirds originated thousands of years ago in China. Another ancient art that has survived into modern times is calligraphy, the production of hand-written messages that are said to bring luck, wealth, harmony and health to anyone who hangs them in their home or office.

The island's architectural heritage includes a wealth of Chinese temples, both ancient and modern. Singapore's first great Buddhist shrine was the Thian Hock Keng (the Temple of Heavenly Happiness), constructed in 1841 by Hokkien immigrants near the spot where they first stepped ashore after sailing from China. A decade later, Teochew settlers built their own waterfront shrine, the Wak Hai Cheng Bio Temple. Both temples are dedicated to the goddess of the sea, not surprising when you consider that both the Hokkien and Teochew were seafaring people. Another important shrine is the Taoist Temple on Kusu Island in the Singapore Strait. Dedicated to the god of prosperity and the goddess of mercy, more than a hundred thousand worshippers make the pilgrimage to the island temple each year, especially those giving thanks for the birth or good health of children. Many of Singapore's most electrifying events—like the Birthday of the Monkey God and Vesak Day (Buddha's birthday)—are best witnessed on temple grounds. A stark contrast to festival time is the quiet, pious devotion that takes place each day in the various Chinese shrines.

Although they comprise less than a sixth of the population, the Malays have left an indelible mark on various aspects of local culture including architecture, language and cuisine. More than any other ethnic group, Malays continue to abide by traditional dress codes and religious rules, and they continue to set aside each Friday as a day of rest, reflection and  prayer at the local mosque. Among the island's most important mosques are the Al Abrar in Chinatown (built in 1850) and the Sultan Mosque in Kampong Glam (1928).

Singapore's association with the Indian subcontinent stretches back thousands of years. In fact, the island's name derives from *singa pura*, an ancient Sanskrit term that means "lion city." Indians were among the first immigrants to Raffles' new colony, many of them merchants and craftsmen who saw the opportunity inherent in a free port under British protection. Although often lumped together, they came from all over the India and embraced many different religions and languages. Many of the later Indian émigrés gravitated towards the police and the civil service, and no small number were originally transported to the island as convict labour to build roads, docks and public buildings. Singapore was ruled as part of British India for much of her earlier history and didn't come under direct administration by the Colonial Office in London  until 1867. Indians now comprise about eight percent of Singapore's total population and Tamil is one of the nation's official languages. Despite their divergent heritage, Singapore's contemporary Indians have one thing in common: a desire to retain the rich vestiges of their past and the customs of their ancestral homeland.

31

Contrary to popular opinion, Little India is not among the ethnic enclaves that Raffles laid out after founding Singapore. During the early half of the 19th century the area harboured rice paddies, sugar cane fields and vegetable plots. By the 1940s, the area was attracting livestock traders, mostly of Indian descent. The Indian population continued to grow and by the turn of the century Little India was flush with shops and services catering to immigrants from the subcontinent. The stables and slaughterhouses were replaced by shophouses and religious structures began to appear. Most notable among the early shrines was Abdul Gaffoor Mosque (1910) and the Sri Veeramakaliamman Temple (1881). Like many of Singapore's historic areas, Little India has undergone extensive renovation in recent years in order to preserve the old shophouses and bygone ways of life. Browsing the neighbourhood you stumble upon goldsmiths and sari boutiques, "banana leaf" curry cafes and shops selling all sorts of Hindu religious paraphernalia, and even parrots that will tell your fortune.

Singapore offers a veritable smorgasbord of Asian cuisine, reflecting the fact that the island's various ethnic groups trace their roots to just about every corner of the continent — China, India and the vast Malay Archipelago. Local food culture runs a broad gamut from traditional street-corner *kopi tiams* (coffee shops) and bustling hawker stalls, to fancy European restaurants, American fast food and sumptuous 12-course Chinese feasts. Food is the national pastime, an infatuation that reflects both the deliciousness of local cuisine and the fact that Singapore is a young nation with few of its own customs and traditions — other than eating. No matter what their career, creed or colour, Singaporeans from diverse backgrounds find that food is something they can talk about and enjoy together, especially at hawker stalls, where taxi drivers, housewives and corporate executives can often be found elbow-to-elbow, discussing the relative merits of a particular dish. Food is even a national symbol — treats like chicken rice, *roti prata* and a pungent fruit called the durian that are as much a part of Singapore's self-image as Orchard Road and the Merlion Statue. Many of Singapore's tourist attractions are also thinly disguised excuses for eating. The Botanical Gardens cultivates some of the city's most romantic eateries while neighbourhoods like Chinatown and Little India offer Asian cuisine within the confines of historic architecture. You can breakfast with feathered friends at Jurong Bird Park or with orangutans at the Singapore Zoo. Indeed, Singapore never seems to run out of eating opportunities.

Architectural renovation and historic preservations have endowed Singapore with some its most atmospheric eating places. Once the home of wealthy Arab merchants, Alkaff Mansion at the summit of Mount Faber in Telok Blangah Park (above) has been restored into an upscale restaurant that offers a mélange of Malay, Indonesian and Western cuisine. Telok Ayer Market (right), erected in 1894 and now the oldest Victorian cast-iron structure in South East Asia, is now a lively hawker centre tucked amid the skyscrapers of the Financial District.

R affles founded the Botanic Gardens in 1822 as an experimental spice farm. Now considered the leading floral showcase in all of South East Asia, the orchid enclosure alone boasts 250 different hybrids or species including the giant Tiger orchid and Singapore's national flower, the Vanda Miss Joaquim orchid. The garden boasts a number of plant oddities including monkey pot trees, a sacred Buddhist plant called the Botree, a 240-year-old cotton plant and a progeny of the rubber tree that gave birth to the Malay rubber industry.

Singapore's Zoological Gardens started life after the Second World War as a menagerie of abandoned British military pets. By the early 1970s it had evolved into a proper zoo, which under the guidance of long-time director Bernard Harrison has developed into South East Asia's most outstanding animal collection. Two of the zoo's primary missions are housing animals in enclosures that replicate their natural habitat and gathering large enough numbers to encourage captive breeding and propagation of the species. The collection boasts animals from around the globe, but its forte is tropical Asian fauna—orangutans, tapirs, sambar deer, Sumatran tigers, hog deer, Indian elephants, sun bear and various monkeys. Free-form natural enclosures are another distinct feature; especially noteworthy are the crocodile, polar bear and hamadryas baboon exhibits, the Komodo dragon habitat and the orangutan island, which has the world's largest breeding group of the endangered orange apes. Surrounding the zoological gardens are the last truly rural parts of Singapore—the vast water catchment nature zone where wild jungle animals still thrive and bucolic areas like Choa Chu Kang and Lim Chu Kang where you can still stumble upon fish farms, orchid plantations, dairy farms and vast Chinese cemeteries with their characteristic womb-shaped tombs.

Jurong Bird Park is a refuge for rare and endangered species of the feathered kind and a wonderful place to learn more about tropical flora and fauna. The park harbours more than 8,000 birds from 600 different species in huge free-flight aviaries and other enclosures that reflect their native habitats. South East Asian birds — like hornbills and birds of paradise — comprise a large part of the population. But there are, in fact, creatures from all around the globe, including Antarctic penguins (housed in a super-cool refrigerated environment), one of the world's largest collections of South American toucans and flamboyant pink African flamingos. Another treat is the nocturnal exhibit, where owls, night herons and the rare New Zealand kiwi lurk in the shadows. Among the Bird Park's other must-see attractions are the world's highest man-made waterfall and largest walk-through aviary. If you're feeling lazy, hop the monorail for a bird's-eye "flight" around the grounds. Those with more energy can follow walking trails that weave between the aviaries and up the flank of Jurong Hill with its panoramic views of western Singapore. There are several shows each day, including one that features chatty acrobatic parrots and another with fabulous birds of prey from around the world. Start the day by having breakfast with birds on the park's Songbird Terrace. Entertainment aside, the Jurong Bird Park is also deeply committed to the propagation and conservation of avian species through captive breeding.

Singapore's "theme park island" is Sentosa, reached via a causeway or cable cars from the west coast. Over the past decade, the Sentosa Development Corporation has ploughed millions of dollars into expanding and improving the island's various attractions. There is literally something for everyone including resort hotels, palm-shaded beaches, golf links, bike trails, aquarium, carnival rides, a  musical fountain, hawker food stalls, a live butterfly enclosure and the superb Pioneers of Singapore exhibit and Surrender Chamber which recount highlights in local history.

S ingapore's national symbol is the celebrated Merlion — a mythical half-fish, half-feline creature emblazoned on coffee mugs, key chains, towels and millions of other souvenirs. According to legend, a Sumatran king was shipwrecked on the uncharted island hundreds of years ago. Scrambling ashore, the royal party spotted an unusual creature with red body and black mane, which they deemed a seagoing lion. Thus was  hatched the Merlion myth. Singapore's most prominent Merlion statues are found on Sentosa Island and at the mouth of the Singapore River.

 Bring your camera—and a sense of humour—when you visit Tiger Balm Gardens on Singapore's west coast. Hundreds of bizarre statues and wacky dioramas make this one of the most offbeat attractions in all of South East Asia. The eccentric Aw Boon brothers, who made their fortune on a popular tropical ointment called Tiger Balm—and who had an acute sense of the absurd—developed the gardens in the 1930s on a property called Haw Par Villa. The result was a fairyland of gaudy plaster scenes inspired  by Chinese legend and great moments in local crime. Among the more gruesome attractions is the 10 Courts of Hell, a ghastly display of people getting their just dues. Other highlights include the Cave of the Spider Women, Romance of the Three Kingdoms, the Dragon Kings and the ever-popular Laughing Buddha, which has become a symbol of Singapore. During much of the 1990s, the gardens were absorbed into Dragon World, a self-styled high-tech mythological theme park that eventually went bankrupt. Nowadays they are open free of charge to the general public.

The Singapore Discovery Centre (SDC) is one of the island's most exciting (and unusual) attractions, an interactive high-tech museum and entertainment centre that showcases the nation's historic milestones and military achievements. Housed in a futuristic V-shaped building on the grounds of the Singapore Armed Forces military training institute in Jurong, the S$70 million facility is striking both in form and content. Looming over the main lobby is a giant photo collage with thousands of typical Singaporean faces, reflecting the nation's multi-cultural heritage. Hallways lead off to various SDC highlights including an interactive talking robot named Little George, a virtual reality sky diving experience, and a motion simulator called *Strike Force* where you get to "ride along" on tank, submarine, helicopter and jet fighter missions. A fascinating historical exhibit on milestones in local history leads into a dramatic three-storey gallery that displays the diverse cultures, achievements and vigour of modern Singapore. Army, navy and air force technology is displayed in a number of ways, including outdoor spaces with military hardware like helicopters and armoured vehicles, a shooting gallery where you can test your proficiency with M16 rifles, and an interactive information gallery with kiosks and games based on military technology. Other rooms are devoted to great armies of the world and "super troopers" — the various missions that modern elite forces like the French Foreign Legion and US Navy Seals are called upon to perform like hostage rescue and parachuting drops behind enemy lines.

Following on a tradition established by Raffles himself, Singapore endures as one of Asia's great marketplaces—although Sir Stamford would hardly recognize "trading" as it's carried out today along Orchard Road (above) and in glitzy, air-conditioned malls like Suntec City (left). Singaporeans have long been enamoured with shopping and there is nothing they would rather do with their free time than window shop and dicker for a good deal. From European haute couture and Japanese electronics  to Indonesian handicrafts and Chinese silks, local stores stock just about everything under the sun.

The slings and arrows of artistic fortune are often aimed at bold modern architecture, but none more so than the Esplanade/Theatres on the Bay performing arts complex in Singapore. The offbeat domes have been a source of much scorn and admiration. Critics have compared the spiky design to everything from giant durians and gargantuan pineapples to punk rock brassieres. "Holy hedgehog!" screamed one local headline. "Are they fly's eyes?" The eclectic complex, built at a cost of US$350 million, embraces a number of performance spaces including a huge main theatre (2000 seats) and concert hall (1600 seats) as well as recital and rehearsal studios, Asia's largest performing arts library, three contemporary art galleries and a massive mall with retail outlets and restaurants. In typical Singapore fashion, no amount of money or effort was spared in transforming the Esplanade into one of the world's top performing arts venues. Every aspect—acoustics, stages, seating and even the dressing rooms—is state of the art. The centre's twin domes are covered by 5,000 triangular panels that block out the sun, help cool the building and give the structure its serrated—and controversial—appearance. Since its first curtain call in 2002, the Esplanade has become a regional hub of drama, dance, music and even comedy.

The nightlife scene largely centres around the waterfront, from world-class symphony within the confines of the Esplanade/Theatres on the Bay (previous pages) to rowdy bars along the banks of the Singapore River. The island's reputation as a rowdy seaport suffered somewhat after independence, when locals got down to the business of nation building. But  in recent years, Singapore has rejuvenated its after-dark revelry by transforming old godowns and shophouses into modern restaurants, bars, nightclubs and performing arts venues.

The International Dragon Boat Festival, which takes place each June on Marina Bay, is just one of many special events that colour the Singapore calendar. The races are inspired by the legend of ancient Chinese poet and public servant Qu Yuan, who threw himself into a river after uncovering widespread corruption and injustice in the imperial court. In  order to keep the fish from devouring his body, local villagers furiously paddled out to the suicide scene and threw rice into the water.

With a cultural heritage that spans four great civilizations—Chinese, Malay, Indian and European—Singapore has more than its fair share of festivals. In fact, nearly every day in Singapore is festive because there's always something special taking place. Events range from local temple festivals in which only a few hundred people take part to nationwide celebrations attended by half a million people. The biggest bash of the year is the two-week Lunar New Year period which culminates in the flamboyant Chingay Parade down Orchard Road, an event unique to Singapore and often described as an Asian version of Rio's famous Carnival parades. But the great thing about Chingay is the fact that all of Singapore's ethnic groups take part—Indians, Malays, Eurasians and Chinese. For local Malays, the most significant time is Ramadan, the Muslim month of prayer and fasting, and jubilant Hari Raya celebrations that follow. Little India is most alive during Deepavali—the Hindu Festival of Lights—which commemorates the victory of good over evil with a dramatic display of night-time lights along Serangoon Road and its side streets. Singapore's biggest secular festival is National Day on 9th August, celebrated on alternate years with a parade along the Padang or in the National Stadium. The display always includes marching bands, military units, cultural troupes and community groups. Wedged between these main events are loads of smaller celebrations and funky little festivals like the Birthday of the Monkey God, the Thimithi firewalking festival, the Dragon Boat Races and the Festival of the Hungry Ghosts.

In the exciting run-up to Lunar New Year, the narrow lanes of Chinatown come alive with the bustle of stallholders selling auspicious plants, fruits and other delicacies. The young "strike it rich" with lucky money called *hongbao* while the adults are encouraged to pay off debts before the new year commences. Among special foods served during the two-week holiday are mandarin oranges, waxed duck and white mushrooms, and a family's Chinese New Year dinner is likely to be the year's most sumptuous feast.

Various ancient Chinese performing arts—some of which are hard to find in China these days—continue to survive and thrive in Singapore. Fukkien string puppets are often trotted out during temple festivals in Chinatown and other ethnic neighbourhoods. Although the art form originated along China's central coast, in Singapore it is often called *"wayang"*—the Malay name for puppets. Although costumes, stage decorations and puppets are based on designs that evolved long ago in China, everything is made in Singapore these days. Chinese opera—especially the Hokkien, Cantonese and Hainanese versions—is another local favourite. During festivals and other special occasions, opera stages are erected in parks, markets and streets, where local opera societies conduct free performances that can stretch for hours or even days. Singapore supports dozens of opera troupes, including prestigious professional companies like the Erwoo Group and the Chinese Theatre Circle. For those who don't speak any of the Chinese dialects, the Chinese Opera Teahouse in Chinatown presents English-language versions of many opera classics.